LADY LEADER

10 Ways to Play in Big Boy Business

by Mary Stier

Mary Stier
13830 Lakeview Drive
Clive, Iowa 50325
© 2011

Cover art by Mark Marturello.

Library of Congress Control Number: 2011916966
ISBN 13-978-1-888223-97-2

"THE REALITY OF THE PAST IS EXCEEDED ONLY
BY THE PROMISE OF THE FUTURE."

— Robert G. Parks, Jr.

—— TABLE OF CONTENTS ——

—— *Introduction* ——

*T*his book has been rolling around my head and heart for three decades.

In the first half of my life I have worked and prospered in a male-dominated industry…the newspaper business. Having been raised in a family with a beloved father, a brilliant mother and two supportive older sisters, the competitive, rough and tumble business world of men was foreign to me. There were very few female role models and so I emulated my male mentors and colleagues. I yearned for a business book that could teach me how to navigate business based on women's unique gifts and strengths. I longed for an encouraging book that taught me how to successfully integrate my personal and professional life. And I searched for knowledge on how to embrace my femininity while still being tough on results.

Left to navigate my career path largely on my own, I lived and learned valuable lessons on attaining a high-profile business career while still being true to myself as a woman.

Each step along the way, I observed, I absorbed, and I learned, and as the greatest Mary of all time did, I "pondered these things in my heart."

So after 25 years I left a glorious media career and started my own company, whose mission is to bring the wisdom and grace of women's leadership into the world. I began teaching, conducting seminars, keynote speaking and executive coaching.

The renewed perspective I received from my students and clients reaffirmed my belief that women share many universal experiences in the workplace. It also became clear to me that the strengths women naturally possess are exactly the leadership skills needed in the new era of today's digital age. Women are wired for communication, collaboration and compassion. Now is the time for women to step up and assume and retain top leadership roles in all industries.

So it is with an open and grateful heart that I am writing this book. Each chapter offers a story from my life, the lesson I learned from that experience and additional resources if you would like to strengthen that specific aspect of your leadership journey. With your busy life in mind, I've distilled the most important ways to play that I learned as a lady leader. We'll explore many topics including power, fear, confidence, clarity and ambition, all through the lens of women's unique experience.

It is my sincere wish that sharing my experiences will enrich, encourage and strengthen you.

All my best,

Mary Stier
September 2011

1
—— BASEBALL VS. BALLET ——

3:39 a.m. I'm awake. The demon has come knocking at the door. Again.

I can't catch my breath. I literally gasp for air. My eyes are open wide and I roll onto my back. It's pitch black in our bedroom, but I can hear Jeff's steady breathing next to me. Have I lost my mind?

How could I even consider taking THE job? That huge promotion in that bigger city?

How could I walk away from…

The first town that ever felt like home?

An envied lifestyle filled with friends and family?

A comfortable paycheck?

My colleagues who came to work for me and with whom I accomplished so much?

How could I even think of…

Asking Jeff to leave his hometown, his job, his friends, his family?

Yanking Ryan out of his preschool and starting all over in a new school system?

Moving my in-laws' grandchild to another city?

3:41 a.m. The thing is, I want this promotion. So here I am in the wee hours, face to face with my ambition.

I know I'm not only good at my job, I'm very good. And I look around this Fortune 500 company and I know that if I choose, I am destined for a position at the top. Not only do I feel it in my gut, my boss is telling me the same thing. He is telling me I can be a player in the newspaper industry.

It's my choice.

3:44 a.m. But when is my ambition detrimental to my family?

3:53 a.m. Why do I feel so selfish being successful?

4:05 a.m. When is enough enough?

Blah, blah, blah. The mind on a hamster wheel keeps turning.

4:16 a.m. But wait—is ambition the demon? Ah ha. It's not the ambition; it's the *fear* of my future that is the demon. I'm realistic about the financial rewards and the value I can bring to the company, but equally aware of the sacrifices it will take to make it in a top leadership position. Are the sacrifices worth it?

4:21 a.m. I want so much to believe the self-help books on my bedside table. The ones that proclaim "Believe, Receive, Achieve."

I give myself a pep talk, trying to convince myself to believe. Yes, yes. I can do it. I CAN do it. I can DO it. I can do IT.

I believe in my ability but am haunted by the enormity of this decision. It will change everything in my life and everything in my family's life. There are no female role models or mentors in my company who are married with children who can offer advice or guidance.

So to whom do I turn?

In the silence of the night, I go to the One who has not left me alone in making this life-altering decision. I slip out of bed and quietly kneel. I go to my God and pray.

Dear Lord, I'm trying really hard to let go and let God. Please show me the way. Show me where I am to be and what I am to do.
Please, just don't let go of me. Just don't let me go.

I crawl back into bed, and the tears fall from my eyes and are silently soaked up on my pillow.

I roll back onto my side and realize how exhausted I feel. There are too many questions and no answers tonight. I have put it all in God's hands. The answers will unfold. But not tonight. All I can do tonight is try and sleep.

7:00 a.m. The alarm goes off. Instinctively, I go through my gratitude list before my feet hit the floor. I get ready in a fog, but with an undeniable sense of peace and confidence.

I am going to say yes to this promotion.

I look in the mirror. I look like shit.

But a piece of shit in Vera Wang.

THE LESSON:

Very few men would put themselves through this amount
of angst when entertaining the thought of a big promotion.
In most cases guys go for it. They just want to be in the
game. Meanwhile, many women politely wait to be invited,
wonder if they have mastered the necessary skills and then
wrestle with complex family issues that often trigger worry
and guilt.

The male CEOs who retain my services for executive
coaching or leadership development services for their staff
inevitably state a variation of the same question: "What is it
with my female leaders? We identify our high-potential
employees, give them access to training and when it's time for
the big promotion, they decline it. What is that all about?"

So I'll ask you the same question. Have you ever seen a
position or been offered a job that really intrigued you,
and you let it slip by? If so, *why?*

Let's start at the beginning.

As far back as the playground, most boys just want to be in

the game. They won't sit back politely and wait to be chosen. Instead, they throw themselves into the center of the activity and vie for position. Being in the game is half the fun.

Years after my angst-filled night, I was reminded of this dynamic when my daughter Emma and I were at a University of Iowa football game. It was a hot September day with the sun baking the football field. None of the players were sitting on the bench gulping down bottles of water. Instead they were all standing along the sidelines intently watching the action on the field.

Emma took this all in and yelled over the thumping of the "Iowa Fight Song," "Do all those players get to play sometime during the season? Or can they go to practice all season but never have the chance to play?"

I nodded to the latter.

And my attention was then diverted to the attractive and painfully thin young women on the dance team, completing a routine on the field in perfect formation. And I saw the metaphor in my own children's lives. It's baseball vs. ballet.

When my son Ryan played baseball as a kid the coach constantly moved him from one position to another to find Ryan's strengths. From outfield to shortstop to first base to catcher to pitcher, back to second base and eventually to playing catcher most games. Ryan was never stressed nor did he feel rejected if the coach moved him to a different position. He was thrilled that he was in the game and trying it all on.

Juxtapose that experience with Emma's ballet lessons. I remember her first recital in her black leotard, pink tights and hair pulled back into a perfect bun.

The girls took the stage and as the lights came up and the music swelled, we saw her in the first row performing each step in perfect unison with the other girls. Success was not winning the game or even participating in it. Instead success was achieved if she didn't make a mistake in the steps she had learned.

Do you see how these early lessons learned as a child can filter into a woman's psyche as she faces her own ambition?

When making life-altering decisions, how much weight is given to avoiding mistakes vs. taking risks to achieve great success? What is the reward ratio between avoiding negative reactions from others vs. allowing one's positive talents to emerge and grow?

A year or so later, Emma gave up ballet and joined a soccer team. She learned about teamwork. She learned that she didn't have to like every team member personally but rather she could value each player for the particular strength she brought to the team as a whole.

When her coach placed her in the coveted goalie position she didn't flinch. She played her heart out.

And when the game ended 2-0 in her team's favor, Emma came off the field, threw her fists in the air and declared, "I am undefeated!"

Yes, guys playing sports at an early age learn how much fun it is just to be in the game, and this lesson easily translates into the business arena.

A woman, on the other hand, often believes she needs to have mastered the skills for the new position before she can apply for it. She believes she needs lots of experience, the MBA or a robust résumé to compete in a larger arena.

Perhaps it is the unrealistic level of perfectionism in our culture that drives a woman to *edit her own ambition* before it can surface.

Meanwhile her male counterpart, who is also interested in this position, raises his hand because it looks intriguing and he just wants to be in the game.

And who gets the promotion? The one who goes for it! So the first obstacle women face is a certain learned reticence when it comes to their own ambition.

The second obstacle women face is waiting to be asked.

I have a client who described her childhood to me. Raised in a very traditional, deeply religious, Southern family, she was taught that girls were to be seen but not heard. Men were waited upon and catered to, while women worked silently in the background. She described these years as "the waiting game…always in hopeful anticipation of being chosen."

Many women are raised to wait and be chosen, instead of learning to choose for themselves.

Have you ever waited to be chosen…for your marriage, your job or a spot on a team?

Again, who gets the opportunity? The one who goes for it!

The third obstacle is fear.

Anytime we make a change in our work life, our personal relationships must adjust. Of course this is true for both men and women.

For a man raised in a culture that demands he provide and protect his wife and children, ambition at any level is valued. In families where the man is the primary breadwinner, there is often an underlying assumption that the family will naturally adjust favorably to any job promotion he receives.

That is not always the case for a woman. For women raised in a culture that demands she is responsible for the emotional well-being of her family, ambition at heightened levels is suspect. A job is different than a highly successful, fulfilling career. When a woman stands at the precipice of the decision—should she go for it, *all* of it, or not?—fear will seize her. She may fear that her marriage may not survive, that her children will not thrive, that she will lose control, that success may spoil her children or harm her own physical or emotional health. With few healthy role models and very little support during her decision-making process, she may decide it's just not worth the risk.

Well, I am here to encourage you to go for it! Whatever it may be in your life. I want you to reach as high as you possibly can. Everything is ok. I promise.

Let me share an idea with you that had a positive impact on me when I felt scared or uncertain or alone.

I had a colleague who was an outstanding executive and who loved to train up-and-coming employees. I had heard rave reviews about her training sessions so I signed up to attend one. I was mesmerized from the start.

She began by having each of us draw a circle and divide the circle into six parts. We labeled each segment of the circle as family, friends, job, spiritual growth, health/recreation and volunteer work. She asked, "In an optimum scenario, how would you like to divide the time in your life in the coming year?" Once we had recorded our desires, she had us pull up our online bank accounts, calendars and emails to see where we were currently spending our time and our money. Well, what I saw was a reversal of my true desires. I was spending the majority of my time at work. Right then and there I had my first wake-up call.

We then took a look at our values…those deep, driving forces in our lives. What values did we hold most dear? Values can include things like achievement, respect, service, integrity, credibility, honesty, family, collaboration, wisdom, generosity and so on. The facilitator asked us to define our top 3-5 values. For me it was the love of my family, serving others and a desire for a healthy lifestyle.

Finally, she had each of us define our greatest strengths. All I knew was that I wanted to grow to be the best leader I could be.

So armed with our true desires on how we wanted to spend our time, our greatest strengths and the values we held most dear, she had each participant write a personal mission statement. Now that sounds a bit daunting, but it's just a concise statement on your life's purpose. What are your dreams and desires? What do you hope to accomplish in your life's work? The mission statement doesn't say how you'll do it. It's not a to-do list or a job description. Instead it embodies your strengths, your passion and your values. It could be 20 words. It could 200. It doesn't have to be perfect.

The key is creating a life's mission statement now that will become your compass as you make decisions in the future.

In my youth I was run ragged by my emotions. After that

exhausting strategy, I realized that I wanted to be guided by my values, not my emotions, when making major decisions. Hence, my life's mission statement:

"With the mutual support and love of my family, I will grow professionally and spiritually to make our world a better place."

In accordance with changing life circumstances, your personal mission statement may change slightly over time, but its fundamentals will most likely remain. Mine has remained the same since I first composed it, and since then I have weighed every major decision in my life against my life's mission statement. Each time an opportunity arrived, whether in my work life or community life, I could view it through the lens of my life's mission statement and decide if it was right. And when everything is aligned? Bingo!

A life's mission statement gives you confidence in making even the most difficult decisions because it is aligned with your value system.

And your family? They will adjust. It may take some time and patience on everyone's part, but change provides all members of the family the opportunity to grow in magnificent ways.

That sleepless night, there was no way I could've known exactly what lay ahead: that today I'd be celebrating my 33rd wedding anniversary with Jeff, that Ryan and Emma would be two extraordinary people who are smart and gifted and kind, that I would enjoy a fabulous 25-year publishing career and would then embark upon a creative life with my own company, that I would enjoy wonderful health and that my relationship with my God would be the strongest ever. But I did know that the extraordinary wasn't going to happen if I edited my own ambition. I knew I had to go for it!

NEXT STEPS:

1) In your journal, make a list numbered 1 through 10. Now list 10 things you have accomplished in your life that give you pride. The next time you want to try something new but hesitate because you believe you need more experience, review this list and see how many things you've accomplished and how many times you jumped in feet first just to give it a try or experience something new.

2) Draw a circle and divide the circle into six parts. Label the segments of the circle as family, friends, job, spiritual growth, health/recreation and volunteer work. In an optimum scenario, how would you like to divide the time in your life in the coming year? Now pull up your online banking accounts, calendar and emails/texts. Where are you spending the majority of your time and money? Are you happy with this? If not what changes would you like to make in the coming year? What would it take to make

those changes?

3) In your journal list the values that you hold most dear.

4) Compose a life mission statement.

5) When have you waited to be chosen? Are you still waiting to be chosen instead of stepping up to the plate? What is holding you back?

6) In your journal, answer this question: What is my greatest fear if I exceed my wildest dreams for success?

7) Do you know a good coach or counselor who can help you break through your fears?

Reading Resources:

On Becoming Fearless by Arianna Huffington

Coaching Into Greatness by Kim George

Necessary Dreams by Anna Fels

Online Resources:

http://www.keirsey.com

http://www.FranklinCovey.com

2
BRING YOUR VOICE INTO THE WORLD

*P*atty was my best friend in 4th grade. She lived several blocks outside our subdivision in a small house behind Katz Drugstore. From a good Catholic family, Patty had eight siblings ranging from high-schoolers to babes-in-arms.

I loved to spend the night at Patty's house.

Compared to the quiet monotony in our household, Patty's home was joyful chaos. Screen doors slamming, kids running in and out, footballs thrown across the TV room, phones ringing, babies crying. It was great.

But I was always a bit self-conscious in their home because I was raised in a quiet household of women. Because my Dad traveled extensively for the Benjamin Moore Paint Company, my mother was charged with raising three daughters, and she ruled the roost with efficiency and order. Our home was uncluttered and disciplined. Patty's house was always in an uproar when her rough and tumble teenage brothers were home. And then there was the tree house.

Nestled up against the edge of the woods her brothers had nailed three planks of wood up onto a tree and constructed a one-room tree house.

It was forbidden territory for a girl to set foot in.

Then late one Friday night, the unthinkable happened. Patty and I were invited up to the tree house to bring her brothers a bowl of popcorn.

I was terrified. As we ascended the ladder and made it onto the rustic floor of the tree house I noticed I was holding my breath. This truly was foreign territory. Cigarette butts were snuffed out on the floor and *Playboy* magazines were tossed about. A dirty sock lay balled up in the corner.

"Well what do you think, kid?" laughed her oldest brother as all her brothers stared at me.

As I opened my mouth, I realized I couldn't speak. I had completely lost my voice.

I bolted for the makeshift ladder, scrambled down the rungs and ran as fast and as far as I could.

Years later, I was invited to join a well known industry board. I wasn't initially nervous when I walked into the building, yet as I entered the first board meeting I had the same sensation I'd had as a young girl in that tree house so many years ago. As I scanned the room I realized I was the only woman in the room.

All eyes were upon me.

Their smiles were a mix of admiration, amusement, bewilderment and in one case, contempt.

But I was no longer a scared girl who wanted to run away. I remembered who I was, what I had accomplished and why I was needed in this organization.

I cleared my throat, smiled broadly and with a confident voice said, "Who brought the popcorn?"

THE LESSON:

Your voice is a muscle. You must use it or you lose it. Fine tune it for powerful results.

When I open my office window at home, I can hear the sound of neighborhood children playing—girls and boys romping in an assortment of games, from tetherball to hopscotch to skateboards to hide-and-go-seek. Their voices, both the boys' and the girls', are clear and full of laughter.

And then at some magical age, sometime between 11 and 14, I notice that the girls' voices are gone.

What are those common threads of what gets in the way of girls and women bringing their voices into the world?

A few years ago I started to pose that question to women and here is a laundry list of their answers:

- Fear – of being rejected, being alone or being without money.

- Worry – about what others will think.

- Insecurity – lack of confidence and not wanting to stand apart.

- Early teachings – to act "ladylike," to be seen but not heard, to take a subordinate role.

- Poverty – lack of access to education or health care.

- Busy-ness – trying to do it all and becoming worn out in the process.

- Dependence – on others, and others on us for protection and security.

- Misplaced focus – on how one looks, taking care of the outside instead of the inside.

- Lack of self-knowledge – not knowing ourselves or discovering our own passions.

Taken together this list is a bit daunting, but somewhere on it I'm sure you have nodded and thought to yourself, "Yes, I understand that one."

So much of what we play out as adults are the messages and meanings hardwired into us as children. Many girls are taught to be polite and to defer to others, while many boys are taught to be direct and assertive.

The best part of growing up is learning to live life to its fullest and learning what is important to YOU.

It doesn't come quickly. Self-knowledge happens bit by bit, piece by piece, until it all comes together like shards of sea glass arranged in a brightly colored mosaic.

So what assists you in bringing your unique voice into the world?

- Discover what you want and have the courage and discipline to focus on it.

- Find friends who support you and support each other.

- Take risks, learn from failures and relish successes.

- Vote.

- Get your education.

- Talk about your dreams.

- Find good health care.

- Give up old stories that no longer serve you.

- Create a full life vs. a busy life.

You can learn these lessons now, but to actually live the wisdom takes a lifetime.

In the meantime, I'd like you to take a look at the following scenario, which you may find all too familiar. I'll then share with you four tips that can help you use your voice in the most powerful way.

Picture this. You, your colleagues and your boss are at your weekly departmental meeting. Overall sales are down and the chief financial officer is sharing the numbers. The tension in the room is palpable, and when the grim report ends, everyone begins to talk at once to give the boss an answer.

You say, "Oh, I'm sorry, Joe. In my experience I think that the customer service department has just finished a new round of training and they have too many new rates in their heads when they're on the phone. So their calls are longer and our customers have to wait too long to get their calls picked up."

No one responds. The conversation continues and about five minutes later Joe says, "Drop-call rates in the call center escalated five percent this week."

Everyone exclaims, "Joe, you're right! Excellent point."

Meanwhile you are fuming as you think, "I just said that. He stole my idea!"

What could you have done to have a stronger voice?

1) Stick to one point at a time.

Because women's brains are wired to hold multiple thoughts at the same time, women tend to weave several interrelated ideas into one statement. If there is a task at hand, men want to focus on the problem, solve it and move on. If you add too many ideas into your statement you appear to be rambling and you lose your audience.

One of the best tips I can pass on to you is this:

When writing an email or text to a male colleague, write one idea per email or text. If you have five ideas, do not put them in one email. Instead write five emails with one idea each. Though at first glance that may seem like an incredible waste of time, I swear it works. You'll get better results if you keep your communications focused, which saves time in the long run.

I have a client who has a very busy boss, and to be respectful of his time she would write one very long email on Friday afternoons with a host of subjects for him to review and on which she needed his feedback. In some cases she needed him to weigh in on a decision that was out of her authority.

And what was his most frequent response to her carefully prepared emails? "OK." Naturally, she was very frustrated by his lack of specific feedback to several complex issues.

At her first review, her boss stated that she needed to have more clarity and confidence in her decisions. I suggested she begin to write him one idea per email and include how she would like him to proceed in all situations. She began to get specific feedback from him and her next review came back with glowing remarks on her strong leadership skills. Stick to one point at a time.

2) Use strong verbs

The first editor I ever hired was Dick Thien. Dick had a passion for teaching journalists the power of language.

He pounded into our journalists in the newsroom the most valuable lesson in communicating:

Power lies with verbs. I witnessed writers getting bogged down with flowery adjectives and adverbs. But it was the writers who understood the power of verbs who had their stories published. I have seen speakers lose their audience with lackluster language. Speak powerful verbs!

In our example above, the first statement to the boss contained weak verbs: am, think, has, have, get.

The second statement had one strong verb: escalated.

Strong verbs are vibrant and powerful. They command attention. They earn respect.

Where do you use written language most often? For some of you it may be in email, online postings or texting. Start there. Look at the verbs you use in communicating every day and challenge yourself to exchange weak verbs with powerful verbs. Start to study public speakers and their use of verbs. Once you get the hang of it, transition your writing of strong verbs into speaking strong verbs. Find a great thesaurus, keep it at your fingertips and use it every day.

3) Don't qualify your statements.
When you have an idea or an opinion, say it.

It's just that simple.

If you qualify the idea by explaining why you believe it (e.g., "In my opinion…" or "In my past experience with such and such organization…") you actually weaken your position.

Qualifying your statements is a form of apologizing. It's as if you are saying, "I am explaining to you why I have the right to speak my opinion."

If you have been invited to the meeting, you have earned the right to speak your voice. Don't qualify your statements.

4) Don't apologize.

My daughter Emma was born to sing. Ever since I can remember, this child has sung. Jeff and I have always known as parents that it is our job to nurture and sustain the gifts and talents within our children. So we sought out a voice teacher to work with Emma.

She took her lessons seriously and diligently practiced for her first recital.

The night before the recital her voice instructor gathered the young singers for a practice run with the piano accompanist.

Emma was up first and was halfway through her song when she forgot a line and then stopped cold and stammered, "I'm sorry. Oh I'm really sorry."

Her voice teacher jumped in. "Ok let's take a break right here because this is an important lesson for all of us. If you miss a beat or forget a line, don't stop and don't say you're sorry. Just plunge ahead and no one will ever notice."

What wise, wise words for all of us.

It takes courage, when one finds her voice, to use it.

And as often happens with women, if we miss a beat or confidence wanes, the next words that follow are: "I'm sorry."

Let's never apologize for our talent or our wisdom or our voice.

And let's take a cue from talented young singers…

Take center stage, take a deep breath and let others hear your unique point of view. It truly is time for all to hear the wisdom and grace of women.

NEXT STEPS:

1) Pull out your journal and look at the first list in this chapter. What has gotten in the way of bringing your voice into the world? Journal on each item that speaks to you.

2) Is there anything that happened in your childhood, apart from this list, that hinders your voice? If yes, have you sought professional help to face it and move forward?

3) Now take a look at the second list. What assists you in bringing your voice into the world? What can you do in

the next month to encourage your voice?

4) Think back over the last six months. Has someone attempted to silence your voice in a group setting? How did you react? Looking back, what would you have done differently?

5) Again, think back over the past six months. Did you use your voice brilliantly? What were the circumstances that gave you confidence and clarity? How can you repeat that practice?

6) Practice using your voice. At the next meeting you attend, make sure you say one thing. At least one thing.

7) Take voice lessons.

8) Make a toast in the next month. Anytime people are gathered around a table to eat, it's time for a toast!

9) If you are terrified of public speaking, take a speech class.

10) Vote!

Reading Resources:

Words on Words by John B. Bremner
The Elements of Style by William Strunk Jr. and E.B. White
Talking from 9 to 5: Women and Men at Work by Deborah Tannen

Online Resources:

http://www.Toastmasters.org
http://www.womensmediacenter.com

3
WHAT DO YOU GET PAID FOR?

A year after I joined the *Iowa City Press-Citizen* as the retail advertising manager we began to get attention from executives in the parent company, Gannett Company, Inc.

Iowa was in the midst of the farm crisis that had rocked the state's economy and shaken confidence.

But at our small daily newspaper in a giant media company we were rocking and rolling. Sales were up 32 percent, and we were getting noticed.

I was asked to attend a meeting for sales managers at corporate headquarters in Washington, D.C. So I packed my best suit, polished my shoes (yes I did), and got ready to "wow" them with my smarts.

My parents were both successful businesspeople in their own right. Dad had a highly successful career with the Benjamin Moore Paint Company and my mother was a thriving entrepreneur. They were thrilled that I was pursuing a business career and they loved to talk business!

So when I returned from D.C. my parents called to see how the trip went.

"So," Mom began, "tell us all the details. How did it go?"

"Oh I think they really like me," I replied. "There were so many people in the room who were afraid to talk. So when they asked a question I volunteered my ideas and told them my opinions. I think they liked that I wasn't afraid to speak my opinion."

There was silence on the other end of the phone line.

Mom took a deep breath. Then she said something that has always stayed with me. "Mary," she said, "they like you because you make them a lot of money."

THE LESSON:

One of women's greatest strengths is our ability to multitask. If not checked, it can become one of our greatest liabilities.

In our quest for meaningful work, in our quest to be liked and in our quest to keep peace we can lose sight of why we were hired and why we are paid.

At that time, my job was to sell advertising. Plain and simple. That's what I was getting paid for.

Over time my responsibilities grew. And each time I started to "wander off the ranch" with some interesting project or new idea I would remember my mother's wise words.

They liked me because I made them a lot of money. That was why I was getting my paycheck.

I've seen local CEOs seduced to serve in community leadership roles who lose sight that their job is to lead their company, not the community. I've seen COOs with strong emotional intelligence get dumped upon with personnel issues. I've seen managers suffocated by playing politics instead of getting their teams to perform at optimum levels.

When a young woman is starting out in her career there are so many things that interest her. And because a woman can multitask at such a high level she can take on a multitude of responsibilities and projects. And a "pile on" can occur. Suddenly she is doing more and more and more while her peers are focused on the job at hand. While her review may state, "She has high energy and is enthusiastic but can lose her focus," her competing peer's review states, "Very focused and exceeds expectations."

Here is a great example from my own career.

I once had a new boss I was anxious to please. He was a rising star and I knew he was well respected. He discovered that I was very good at conducting sales audits within sales operations. In other words, I could go into a sales department and within a couple of days I could assess the operation top to bottom, pinpoint weak areas and make meaningful recommendations on how to improve the sales.

Obviously this is a very useful skill within a sales operation. In fact, companies spend some pretty hefty fees to hire consultants to do just this.

My new boss called me one day and said, "Mary, I have a great opportunity for you. I'd like you to assemble a small team and conduct sales audits at all 15 of my newspapers. It will require that you travel for five weeks but it will expose you to 15 different markets. I'd like you to lead the team and personally lead these audits." And the kicker?

I was still responsible for all my duties as publisher of my own newspaper and I had a very green team in place.

My gut was telling me that this project was the equivalent of adding another full-time job onto my schedule while I was currently facing the challenges of leading an inexperienced team at my home newspaper. However I knew it would be a feather in my boss's hat and I was determined to show him that I was a player on his team. I told my boss I'd be happy to take on the task.

Well, the sales audits were a great success but at my newspaper, with no seasoned boss at the helm for five weeks, my own operation slipped. The next kicker? My annual bonus was based on the performance of my home newspaper, not on special projects. What should I have done differently?

1) I should have negotiated some time to think through the project and its impact on my primary job. With a little bit of distance I could have clearly thought through my boss's

expectations and the resources needed to reach his anticipated outcomes.

2) Once I knew the resources required I should have negotiated additional support for the sales audits so that I could still remain focused on my core job. Here is where we can learn from our male colleagues. More often than not when a woman receives a project at work she accepts it at face value and does not negotiate any support to help her accomplish the goal. Instead of asking for support she thinks, "Yes, I can do that project. It may take another couple of hours per day—I'll just work weekends or get to work earlier!" You think I'm joking but it happens every day. In contrast, when given the chance at a high-profile project our male colleagues will typically respond, "This is terrific, Chief! I would love to have a chance to work on that project and make this a great success for you. I'll just need 20 hours of additional clerical help each week to get the project in tip-top form." This response opens the door for negotiating resources. If the boss doesn't want to commit additional resources to the project then chances are he or she isn't expecting huge rewards from the project or it's really not at the top of his or her priority list. Your time and talent are an investment. Don't give them away.

3) If you really want to do the project and the boss won't commit to more resources, determine how critical the

project is to achieving your long-term goals. Get very clear on this. If it's interesting but not getting you closer to your goals, let someone else have the project. If it seems worth the additional work, articulate the potential impact it could have on your day job. Set up a project timeline and check in with your boss for progress reports on all your areas. The mantra? No surprises!

4) As uncomfortable as it may be, talk about compensation. Will you be compensated for this special project? If not, how much would the company pay a consultant or hire a freelancer to accomplish this project? Leverage this information to negotiate fair compensation for your work. If you will be compensated, how and when will you be paid?

5) If you are the "go to" person for a boss who has a tendency to "pile on" the project work, you need to set a boundary. You can easily do this by reminding your boss of all the projects on your plate: "This new project sounds great. As a reminder I have the following projects in process. If this is a priority, which project would you like me to table or hand off to someone else to make this new project a priority?"

This gets your boss focused on priorities, requires him or her to make a decision and helps clarify what is most important in his or her world.

It's your job to know your responsibility to the company and understand when a special project could ultimately interfere with what you get paid for. It is also your responsibility to say "no" when the special projects will get too distracting or take you away from your primary and vital role.

Burnout is very real, and a serious result of multitasking gone awry.

This valuable lesson at an early stage in my career taught me to be very clear on my responsibilities. It also taught me to negotiate the time, resources and money associated with special projects.

As my father advised me long ago, "No one knows your value until you tell them."

In closing, remember this: Just because you are good at it doesn't mean you have to do it. Stay focused on your long-term goals.

NEXT STEPS:

1) Sit down with your boss and ask the question, "What does the company pay me for?"

   Listen carefully. Clarify.

   With this information in hand, look at your calendar and your emails/texts and see how much time you spend on the activities that help you reach the goal of what you are paid for.

Look at the activities that are keeping you from accomplishing the goals that the company or institution needs to deliver.

Look at your activities again. What activities energize you? What activities deplete you? Are you taking on projects to fulfill your creative juices but that are taking you away from your main work? Is there a way you can get more of those creative projects to be part of your official job description?

2) Take a look at your compensation package, both salary and bonus. Are you being fairly rewarded for the special efforts you are putting forth? If not, will you commit to negotiating fair compensation terms prior to a project?

3) What is your real motive for accepting special projects? Acceptance from the boss? Recognition? Learning new information or skills? Networking opportunities?

Are the special projects fulfilling you more than your responsibilities of what you get paid for? If yes, what would your dream job be? How can you move closer to this destiny?

Reading Resources:
Boundaries by Dr. Henry Cloud and Dr. John Townsend
How to Say It for Women by Phyllis Mindell

Online Resources:

http://www.wageproject.org

http://www.sabonline.com

http://www.karrass.com

4
—— LIVING IN DISNEYLAND ——

*I*t was the big board in town. All the movers and shakers were on it and all the up and comers aspired to serve on it. So when I got the call that they wanted me to serve on the Board of Directors, and get paid for my services, I thought I had arrived.

In anticipation of attending my first meeting I scoured the agenda and plowed through all the reading material. This was going to be great!

The board room was on the top floor of a modern skyscraper downtown. It was opulent...a Persian rug over polished floors, black leather chairs, engraved mahogany board table and Waterford crystal glasses on the credenza.

Each board member was placed around the table in alphabetical order.

The new Chairman arrived and worked the room, greeting each board member with a quick handshake. He smiled broadly and welcomed me to the board.

We all sat down and the meeting began. Within minutes the topic abruptly turned to an article that had been published in the newspaper three days prior. The Chairman's anger erupted and locking eyes with mine, he unleashed a bitter monologue on how the newspaper had been in error. I knew otherwise.

All eyes were upon me when he finished his outburst.

All waited to see how I would react.

I smiled. My eyes twinkled, on the verge of a wink.

"Oh Mr. Chairman," I said, "you know better than to pick a fight with a woman who buys newsprint by the ton and ink by the barrel!" And then I laughed.

There was five seconds of silence and then the room erupted with laughter.

Including the Chairman.

Armed with a sense of humor, I had won the first round.

THE LESSON:

In male-dominated industries, men are encouraged to jockey for a position of power. In interactions they look for an advantage, vie for the best position and keep score. Women, on the other hand, tend to seek balance in an exchange.

It all begins on the playground.

With pent-up energy from being confined to a desk and chair, boys spill out onto the playground, arms and legs pumping to find a game to play. They grab a ball to throw, a stick to pitch or another friend to wrestle to the ground. Life is a game and they want to play it. But they learn very early that on the playground someone wins and someone loses. And it is just human nature that they do not want to be the loser. At this point the physically strong and confident boys emerge as the winners. And an invisible hierarchy is formed from top to bottom in the class.

Boys learn very early to jockey for position with the goal of being the highest man on the totem pole—and to avoid at all costs being in the lowest position.

Boasting is one of winning's by-products.

I once heard a story about a mom who picked up her young son and a friend after school. Her son and his friend were discussing spring break plans. Her son delighted in announcing to his friend, "My family is going to see my grandma next week." Her son's friend eagerly responded, "My family is going to Disneyland!" Her son, not able to stand being one-upped, fired back with, "Well my family is going to LIVE in Disneyland!"

Now let's return to the playground and observe girls.

As girls are released onto the playground, they tend to cluster in small groups. They keep their best friends close by to discuss important matters. Their goal is to build relationships and they do this through intensive verbal communication.

So what happens when these early, reinforced behaviors encounter each other in the workplace?

Time and time again when a business gathering is composed of a majority of men, jockeying for position occurs. It first shows up in non-verbal communication.

In your mind's eye picture a conference room with a rectangular table in the center of the room. Traditionally the most powerful person will sit at the head of the table. At the opposite end sits the second most powerful person in the room. Sitting to the right of the top leader will be the leader's go-to person and to the left will be his or her personal ally. The peacekeeper in the group will sit at one of the middle seats.

Before anyone has said a word, jockeying for position has occurred. Choosing where one sits at a table tells others about one's perceived role, one's relationships and one's intent for the interactions during the meeting.

Then, once everyone has chosen a place to sit, the chitchat starts. Immediately, the differences in the way men and women interact are apparent. As the women gather they may notice what another woman is wearing and comment, "Jessica, I love those shoes. Where did you get them?" Now I have never seen a male compliment another man on his appearance. Instead, I have seen men use humor to playfully jockey for a higher position. Your male colleague might say, "Dan, that is the ugliest tie I have ever seen in my life.

Was Goodwill having a two-for-one sale this weekend?"

It has been my observation that men often come into an exchange with the goal of elevating their position and status. They will arrive at a meeting with an idea and focus their energy on positioning that idea as the best in the room. On the other hand I have observed women eliciting many viewpoints, including those of their subordinates, in order to formulate suggestions and ideas or to round out an idea as it is being discussed. Now obviously men also value input and women also like to sell their ideas. However men and women can get caught in the crossfire with each other because they misinterpret the other's motives. Neither wants to be perceived as arrogant, or on the flip side, weak. Neither wants to be pushed around or pushed down to a lower role. Both have the goal of finding the best solution. They just approach it differently.

If you watch a person's verbal and nonverbal language it's pretty easy to figure out his or her motive in any interaction with others. But what I've learned is that where most people get tripped up is in their *response* to the tactics used by others to gain a more favorable position.

Overt power plays tend to elicit an immediate strong response. Depending on your personality you may get angry and push back, or you may hold in your response and grow resentful. Neither is a particularly successful strategy.

Whether the power plays on your team are overt or of a subtler nature, the most important guidance I can give is threefold:

Expect it.

Don't take it personally.

And bar none, the best response is humor. Humor is the great equalizer.

One last thing, however: remember that there is a dark side to any quest for power.

It's called the bully.

The first type is the overt bully. You met him or her on the playground and they haven't changed in all these years. The overt bully must exert force to win and must win at all costs.

Does any of the following sound familiar?

They over-control.
They micromanage.
They openly display contempt for others.
They exploit employees.
They humiliate others.

The second kind of bully is the excluder. You knew him or her as the mean kid who pulled friends in tightly and terror-ized others by excluding them from information and activi-ties. This more subtle kind of bully must lead the charge in ostracizing others in order to win.

They gossip.
They label.
They foster exclusivity.
They belittle.
They manipulate.
Both types of bullies abuse power.

If you work for or with a bully here are some tactics that work:

1) Address the behavior immediately. If you do, the bully will move on. If you don't you will become the punching bag.

2) Confront the bully, but do it in private. If you confront the bully in public he or she will become very threatened and will lash out at you.

3) Be specific. What behavior is unacceptable? State clearly that you will not put up with this specific behavior.

4) Try humor to defuse an emotional confrontation. Remember the bully's goal is to control others and win at any cost.

5) Build your network. Surround yourself with allies.

Make sure your bosses' boss knows of your great results and positive performance.

Early on in our childhoods we learn what behaviors are rewarded.

Teachers praise the child whose inclusive personality softens a rift among peers and who finds common ground among classmates.

Teachers praise the child whose confidence rallies classmates to action.

Do you see how the affirmation of these roles can transpire in the workplace years later?

Men are raised to look for an advantage, jockey for a better position and then to keep score in an interaction, while women are raised to balance the power in an exchange.

Neither is right nor wrong. Instead, let's learn from each other and find the best of both approaches in our highly competitive culture.

NEXT STEPS:

1) Begin to watch the interactions of your team. Who always positions themselves to win an exchange?

2) How do you react when a colleague moves to put himself/herself in a superior position? Are you reacting or responding?

3) Do you have a bully in your life? Have you confronted him or her?

4) Who uses humor in your life to deflect awkward situations? What can you learn and when can you practice the power

of humor?

5) What is your greatest source of humor? A favorite
   comedian? A favorite actor or actress? A favorite author?
   A website with humorous videos? Take time each week
   to expose yourself to a good belly laugh. Practice using
   humor in your exchanges in your professional and
   personal life. It's just plain fun!

Reading Resources:

Survival of the Savvy by Rick Brandon and Marty Seldman
The Definitive Book of Body Language by Allan and Barbara Pease
What Got You Here Won't Get You There by Marshall Goldsmith

Online Resources:

http://www.wallstreetjournal.com
http://www.forbes.com
http://www.nbc.com/saturday-night-live

5
—— POWER ——

*A*fter working hard for 18 years and earning my stripes in smaller markets I was asked to assume the top leadership role as president and publisher at the *Des Moines Register*. I was delighted to return to a state that always felt like home. And thrilled to take the helm of a newspaper that I always respected.

Over the years people often remarked of my vocation, "I would never want THAT job." The intensity and scrutiny were certainly not for the fainthearted.

But the newspaper business suited my personality. The environment is filled with creative characters driven by the adrenaline of deadlines, and dreamers determined to right the wrongs in our country. I fit right in.

I was born with a dual gene—a dreamer with a head for business. Newspapering is a business, but one that stands in the doorway of democracy. You have to make money to make that work. We conducted business so we could do what we loved.

John Quinn, a beloved former executive vice president for news in Gannett, used to say it was our inner poet that kept us striving to serve the institution. That inner poet sustained me as my newspaper career advanced and I ultimately became the philosophical and business leader for 35 newspapers in Midwestern and Southern states.

It was also that dream that drew me to the *Des Moines Register*. I relished the *Register*'s storytelling, photography, art, editing, kick-ass reporting, lively opinions and the voice that championed the people of Iowa.

So when the company asked if I would move to Des Moines and take the helm as the president and publisher of the *Register* I jumped at the chance.

Each time I moved into a new community as publisher of the daily newspaper it was an eye-opening experience.

Every community had an "A-list" of power brokers. Every place had an unspoken set of influences that drove the engine in the community.

In Iowa City, Iowa, home of the Hawkeyes, the engine was naturally the University of Iowa.

In Rockford, Illinois, Chicago politics was king and naturally, the engine was elected politicians.

In Des Moines, Iowa, home to several industry captains, the engine was business.

And in most communities the majority of power resided in a small group of white, middle-aged men. Many of the social structures of the community were exclusive and difficult to break into. Young men and women aspired to gain entry into breakfast clubs, service organizations and top country clubs.

So imagine the difficulty of conducting business as a young woman in a leadership position when these organizations barred women from entering. For many in the Millennial generation that seems so long ago that it's not even a relevant issue to discuss. And yet when I started as publisher not so long ago in Iowa City, Iowa, the Rotary club did not have female members. In Rockford, Illinois the most prominent country club did not accept female members and in Des Moines, Iowa, the most prominent business breakfast club did not have a single female member.

Part of my personal philosophy is that in business, relationships are king. When a roadblock appears that hinders a member of my team or me from building strong relationships, I will look for a new avenue or idea and strive to break through that barrier.

Exclusion, whether overt or subtle, is one of the most damaging roadblocks, and it's a power play.

If you face this challenge today or in the future, your job is to find a different path resulting in your desired outcome while still retaining your personal power.

Here is a story to illustrate the point.

When I was named publisher in Iowa City I had lived and worked in the community for 13 years. I had long-standing relationships with university and business leaders and could build on those to accomplish the goals of the organization.

When I was named publisher in Rockford I had two bosses who had previously lived in Rockford and who personally introduced me to key community leaders, who in turn opened doors for me in building relationships.

Then I arrived in Des Moines. I didn't know a soul in the business community and the silence was deafening. Not to be deterred, I knew it was up to me to build those relationships person by person. But where to begin? I asked the editor of the newspaper to assemble a group from the newsroom to share their thoughts and knowledge on the history of the community and its most influential community leaders.

About 10 journalists sat around a table and thoughtfully answered my questions. At the end of the hour I asked each of them to name the most powerful leaders in the community. As each person answered the list became quite clear. The last to answer was a long-time, respected editor. He took a moment, looked me straight in the eye and said, "Most powerful leader?" A slight smile crossed his lips. "You're the president and publisher of the *Des Moines Register*. You are."

THE LESSON:

Never, ever give your power away and wait for it to be given back to you. It's your power.

Have you ever given your power away? To your boss? To your company? To your partner? To your parents? To your children? To your best customer? To an addiction?

The tragedy for me is when I see people give their power away so often that the behavior becomes the norm. When that happens, they become the people someone else wants them to be instead of becoming their authentic self.

In rigid, hierarchical environments, power can have a different definition for men than for women.

It took me a while to figure this one out. I believe it was because I was raised in a tightly knit family of strong women and then entered a male-dominated field. There, it didn't take long for the male model of power exhibited in business to become my new norm.

The modeling behavior that was rewarded was to exert control over others. Intimidation, temper tantrums and verbal abuse were acceptable and even expected forms of leadership. I tried it on a few times and it was so foreign to me that I knew I was being untrue to myself, not to mention that it was not building healthy relationships with my colleagues or employees.

In the book *See Jane Lead* Lois Frankel says it best when she observes, "Whereas men often define being powerful as getting someone else to do what they want or having control over others, women tend to define it as getting to do what they want or having control over themselves."

When do you feel powerful? When you are true to your values and to your leadership style?

I had to ask myself those questions when I realized that the modeling behavior I was trying on wasn't a good fit at all. I realized that for me, my number-one value is growth. It's when I am growing people, institutions and my own development that I am most powerful. Let me illustrate this point.

When I first was given the responsibility of overseeing a group of newspapers in tough, cold Midwestern towns it became very clear early on that my competitors would recruit our best talent away to attractive, warm and growing markets. So I consciously built a culture of identifying high-potential talent within our group and developing them. We were honest with those we were recruiting by telling them we didn't have sexy things to sell like mountains or beaches, but if they wanted a place where they could grow personally and professionally we would help them reach their goals. And they came. We offered more training hours per employee than any other division or region in our company. The training programs we created were not only modeled throughout the Gannett Company, but they created a new generation of leaders.

And here is the bottom line. They produced outstanding results. Our region, with the toughest economy in the nation at the time, outperformed the company division and the industry averages consistently for over a decade.

At the time, the way to get ahead in the company was to move up through smaller markets until one reached a metropolitan operation. Having been raised in a family that moved every few years, I knew of the wear and tear that relocation can force on families. I knew we had exceptional talent in the group but there were individuals who had been overlooked because they chose not to relocate. What a waste of potential talent! So in our leadership development programs we openly talked to employees about advancement. We communicated that if they could relocate, advancement would happen quickly. However, if they chose to stay in their hometown and we invested development dollars in them, we would ask them to become an expert in their field and we would call upon them to share their knowledge and expertise at our other newspapers. They embraced this model wholeheartedly and we built a network of seasoned experts in all aspects of our business operations. Putting my value of growth into action allowed me to step into my power in a meaningful way.

Now what does power look like? It sometimes comes in unexpected guises.

By my good fortune I worked in a company for 25 years that walked its talk when it came to diversity. Young, old, black, white, male, female...all had powerful roles in the company. All that mattered was that you got results. Yet when I went out into my community as a young leader I was met with bewilderment. I'm a petite and polite woman. Add youth to that one and some people didn't take me seriously. You can't control what people think of you initially but you can affect your power by living a life of integrity, keeping your word and getting results.

Also, when I entered corporate life I observed how important symbols of status were in the allure of power. The corner office, the performance car, the membership at an exclusive club, the corporate jet, the best seats in the stadium...all perks and symbols of power. As God as my witness, I have seen grown men almost get into fistfights over six inches of office space. If you want to stress out a player, reduce their real estate.

Now I like nice things just like other people. But the acquisition of them doesn't drive me. That said, symbols of power are strong currency in business, and I have learned to respect them and accept them.

Case in point: I have a client who was promoted to the vice

president level who could care less about the new office with a view and who truly preferred to stay in her cubicle next to her team. It wasn't until I explained that her peers would view this as a weak move and her staff would believe she had less power because she had not accepted the gift of real estate that she graciously embraced the status symbol of her new office.

The bottom line, of course, is that all the outward signs of power pale in comparison to what actually makes you powerful: living your values, getting results and living a life of personal and professional integrity. You can surround yourself with the symbols of power but we all know that substance over form must occur in order to be a truly powerful person.

When you are first beginning to feel your power it can be intoxicating. It's often when one flexes one's muscles and begins to comprehend one's influence over others. Unfortunately some leaders get stuck in this space and never move forward. You may have been deemed powerful by way of your position but positional power is shallow and shortsighted. Real power occurs when one moves from positional power to personal power.

Personal power is achieved by fine-tuning these qualities: unwavering self-knowledge, leading for results and influencing others for the greater good.

Through it all you must embrace and protect your power. The more power you have the more others will attempt to snatch bits and pieces of it to call their own. It's important to share the leadership journey with others, but how do you know when others aren't worthy of your power?

Watch what others do with the power you give them. If they hoard it or lord it over others their intentions are not pure. If they in turn share it with others and attempt to improve the lot they have been given, they are on their way to becoming a powerful leader.

So you see, you give power to grow others and institutions, and eventually it will result in growing yourself. But never, ever give your power away to someone or something and wait for it to be given back to you. It's *your* power.

NEXT STEPS:

1) Do you ever give your power away and wait for it to be given back to you? To whom or what? Why?

2) When do you feel powerful?

3) What is your number one value? How can you incorporate this value into your leadership vision and act on it every day?

4) Do you embrace communication, collaboration and compassion in your leadership style? How can you live the

more fully each day?

5) What are the symbols of power in your organization? List them and who has them. What are the common themes? If your peers all have a perk (e.g., membership in a club) and you don't, inquire when this can change.

Reading Resources:

See Jane Lead by Lois Frankel

Standing at the Crossroads by Marian Ruderman and
Patricia Ohlott

The Servant Leader by James Autry

Online Resources:

http://www.marystierconnects.com

http://www.theglasshammer.com

6
——SIMPLY ELEGANT——

*G*rowing up as the third girl with two older sisters, I got a lot of "hand-me-down" clothing. Because my mother was a talented seamstress, it really wasn't so bad... except the year my mom insisted I wear my eldest sister's red mohair sweater when the itchy yarn had been out of style for five years. The taunts at school were pretty harsh.

So when I started earning a real paycheck I discovered the joy of buying new clothes. What a great vice!

The first time I anted up $200 for a professional business suit I literally calculated the return on investment right there in the dressing room. I asked myself, "How many times a year will I wear this suit? How many years will I wear it? Therefore, how much will it cost each time I wear it?" After the quick analysis I gave myself permission to buy it. And I was off and running with my personal love affair with fashion.

When I started my business career in the liberal college town of Iowa City, Iowa, women's professional fashion was pretty low-key. My nondescript suits fit in just fine.

Then I moved to Rockford, Illinois. One wouldn't think a factory town such as Rockford to be a place of high fashion, but surprisingly, its proximity to Chicago does have influence on its fashion sense.

Not that I knew that at the time. So I packed up my $200 suits, oxford shirts and silk bow ties and set off for my adventure. On the first day of the job, as I was being introduced to the executive team, I noticed that all of them were impeccably dressed. One of the female executives was hard not to notice in a Donna Karan knit dress, Donald Pliner pumps and Chanel jewelry. I made a mental note to get her advice on great places to shop.

Early in my tenure as president and publisher of the *Rockford Register Star*, the two of us scheduled a day together so that she could give me a retail store tour.

Our first stop was the Saks store.

"Do you have personal shoppers on the floor today?" she asked, with just enough impatience to get their attention.

"Why of course," answered the sales associate. "What are you shopping for?"

"Women's suits," she replied.

"My pleasure," replied the sales associate. "Andrea will assist you. Please follow me."

On the third floor we were greeted by Andrea, who offered us wine, water or coffee. We waited in comfortable chairs until Andrea returned with our bottles of water, and then my colleague informed her that I was in the market for a new suit. Andrea took me by the arm and quietly said, "Come with me."

She chose several suits, hung them in a spacious dressing room and asked me not to pass judgment on the suit on its hanger, but instead to try on each one and come out to model them.

I picked a classic navy suit with subtle white trimming and crisp, classic buttons. As I took it off the hanger and looked at the label I mused, "I have never seen a St. John suit before."

Once the suit was on, I turned and looked at myself in the mirror.

The suit fit perfectly, as if it had been made for me. Andrea knew her stuff.

Then I looked at the price tag. And gasped.

I felt a bit of nausea. My mind raced. Who in their right mind would spend that kind of money for a jacket? But I couldn't get out of this now—I at least had to model the suit.

When I rounded the corner my face must have shown my delight with the transformation but hesitation at the price.

With broad smiles, Andrea and my new colleague looked at me and then at each other. Andrea declared, "You will command a room when you wear that suit."

As I turned and looked in the mirror a thought crossed my mind: "You are the publisher of the newspaper. Step up to the plate and look the part." Priceless.

I bought not one but two suits that day and never looked back.

THE LESSON:

If you are to be given the respect you deserve you must dress the part.

There is an old saying that "clothes make the man." Well I am here to tell you that clothes make the woman, too.

For a man, dressing for success is ready-made. Depending on the culture of a company, it's pretty darn basic—a suit, slacks or classy jeans. A guy takes one look at how the CEO is dressed and emulates his boss.

But women have far more variety than men, which makes things a bit more complicated, but infinitely more fun. The key to dressing for success for a woman is this: find your style.

Your style.

It took me a very long time to find my style. I have always envisioned myself as an artist of sorts so when I entered the world of business I was at a bit of a loss as to how to dress. The "dress for success" books I consulted basically took a man's suit and added a skirt, pantyhose and a silk bow tie.

I couldn't mesh my personal vision of myself with the standard fare they touted, and as a result my closet was filled with confining, generic clothes that restricted me and didn't convey who I was at my core.

I want you to think about the women in your work life. What does their fashion style convey?

Have you seen women try to appear more powerful by wearing grossly oversized jewelry?

Have you seen women cloak themselves in loosely fitting clothes in an attempt to be invisible?

Have you seen women dressed like men who just want to fit in with their male colleagues?

On the flip side, have you watched a woman enter the room, one who you instinctively know is powerful? What was she wearing?

Do you know a woman who lights up a room with her presence, poise and self-confidence? What is her style?

Yes, your performance at your job is ultimately more important than style, but your style is an instant, incredibly powerful nonverbal cue to everyone at the workplace. Your style immediately conveys who you are and where you are going so you need to define it, build it and wear it.

Let me share a story about how I found my style. That day at the Saks store I'd made the commitment to investing in my wardrobe, but admittedly, even a couple of years later I still had room to grow. I wanted to do a better job of building a wardrobe for the long run. I was tired of "drive-by shopping"—stealing a moment or two to shop for clothes that were too trendy and didn't last two seasons.

I wanted to open my closet at 5:30 a.m. half asleep and pick three things that would always work together.

And I wanted to stay within a budget.

So I asked for help. During a visit with my dear friend Denise Ivey in Pensacola, Florida, Denise took me to see Sarah Brown, who owned, in my opinion, the most incredible women's clothing store on the face of the earth.

A block from the waterfront, Sarah's store immediately filled your senses with colors, textures and beauty. Designers such as Vera Wang, Armani, Max Mara, Alberta Ferrini and Calvin Klein graced tasteful displays.

Now I'm not a shopper. To tell you the truth I'm a bit overwhelmed by the choices and never know where to start.

Sarah, however, was a master. As I conveyed my needs, she asked a very simple question: "Of all the women in the world, whose style do you most admire?"

Two names came to mind: Jackie O. and Audrey Hepburn.

Then she asked, "How would you define their style?"
And two words instantly came to me: Simply elegant.

I could finally articulate it! It was my intention to have a
wardrobe that was simply elegant.

Sarah padded about her store and brought me several
options for building my wardrobe from scratch. Each time
I emerged from the dressing room, she skillfully adjusted a
hemline or pulled in a seam so I could envision a perfectly
tailored skirt or pair of pants. Then she paired a belt or
a scarf or a necklace, draping the accessory effortlessly to
complete the ensemble.

And as she worked quietly, tilting her head in deep thought,
vanishing for a moment only to reappear with an item that
completely changed the look of the outfit, I looked in
the mirror.

With Sarah's help, I could see not only who I was at that
moment but who I would grow to be.

That's when I realized that it was possible to express my
authentic self through the gift of fashion.

And that is what I want for you.

You are one of a kind. You are strong and talented and smart
and capable of great things. You must convey that each day
when you face the world.

So you need a signature style. And only you can define what that style is for you.

Once you define your style you can begin to build the basics of your wardrobe. What do you need?

Here is a list that can set the stage for your wardrobe:

- Black pants that fit your body type
- Pencil skirts in solid or neutral colors
- Fun blouses that fit your personality
- A classic white shirt
- The little black dress
- The power suit
- Tailored neutral jackets
- A pair of fitted jeans
- One great pair of black shoes and one great pair of neutral shoes
- A striking handbag
- Two unique belts
- A classic coat
- A few pieces of beautiful jewelry

And here are some basic rules I've learned along the way that I'll pass on to help you define your style and build your wardrobe:

1) Classic forms (the pencil skirt, the boyfriend jacket) are best to build your wardrobe foundation.

2) Build with basic lines and enhance with color and texture.

3) Get a good tailor. Your clothes should fit you as if they were personally made for you.

4) Always look for proportion and scale for your body.

5) Go for comfort. If you are pulling or tugging your clothes it will distract you as opposed to helping you feel confident and powerful.

6) Accessories update you and enhance your style. Pass up quantity and go for quality. If your basics are the cake, your accessories are the icing.

7) Don't wait for weight. In other words don't wait to build your wardrobe until you have lost that magical number of pounds that you have in your head. You are competing today so start today.

8) Don't wait to win the lottery. You can build a great wardrobe on a limited budget by shopping cool websites and store sales. Tasteful, elegant clothes need not be expensive.

I have colleagues who are known for always wearing high heels or a big ring or unique belts. I have friends who always wear skirts and others who wear trim pants. But it's their style and it fits their personality like a glove. Is there a signature style in your wardrobe? If not, then you have the potential to fade into the woodwork with everyone else.

Before we move into "next steps" on how to define your style, I have a few words of caution.

Unless you are a rock star or movie star, never, and I mean never, show cleavage or wear a tight, short skirt in your work environment. You may have a body to kill for and work hard to keep it that way, but if you are to be taken seriously in a leadership role you can't expose your body in inappropriate ways.

As women we are held to a different standard. I wish it weren't the case, but it is. It's been that way for thousands of years and I don't see it changing anytime soon.

Men naturally find us attractive. Honestly, it doesn't take much for them to fantasize about the woman sitting next to them right now. If you are showing cleavage or your skirt is inching up your thigh, the man you are talking to is not listening to a word you are saying. He is thinking about sex. With you.

This is wonderful if it's your husband or partner. It's not good news if it's your boss, your colleague, your employee, your customer or your client. Dressing sexy might make you feel attractive and it may seem like good, clean, flirty fun, but it's going to hurt you in the long run. It defines your style as sexual and minimizes how successful and smart you are at your core.

And it doesn't take much to cross the line from tasteful to tasteless.

Here is the test. If you wear an outfit that attracts attention to your skin and not to your brain, wear something else to work.

A woman's sexuality is very powerful. Your sexuality is a meaningful part of your personal life. Keep it there. Not in the workplace.

Finding your style and building your wardrobe can be a powerful ally in your career advancement.

Of course, clothes will never substitute for competence, ability or results, but they will convey your image. And you want to convey your smarts and your confidence.

It's all about confidence. Nothing is sexier than a woman who knows herself, is comfortable in her skin and has the confidence and courage to face whatever life throws at her. Trust me, guys would kill for this advantage!

It's your advantage (and a fun one at that!) so step up to the plate.

NEXT STEPS:

1) Define your personal style! Go to the newsstand and peruse all the fashion magazine covers. Pick a stack and

take them home. Thumb through each magazine and every time you see a look, an outfit or an accessory that attracts you, rip the page out and set it aside. Take these pages and lay them all out in front of you. What are the common themes? What keeps showing up? If you had to define the style, what would you call it? Ask yourself, what do I want others to think based upon my appearance and what do I want to instantly convey?

2) Invite close friends over whose style you admire and ask them to help you. Show them the pages from your magazine tour, articulate your style and then have them help you "edit" your closet. Try every item on in your closet and let them give it a thumbs-up if it stays, a thumbs-down if it goes and a neutral if you can't decide. For the items that stay, organize them and then see what is missing to complete your wardrobe. For the items that go, donate them or give them away. For the clothes designated for the neutral pile, put them in a bag and let them sit for six months. If you haven't pulled them out in that time, get rid of them.

3) Make an appointment at your favorite fashion store. Just about every store has a personal shopper who can help you pick items and won't charge for the service. Be candid with the personal shopper about your style, your goals and your budget. If the personal shopper isn't a good listener,

is too pushy or you don't connect with him or her, move on. Find someone you trust who has your best interests at heart. Once they get to know you they will call with items that would work well for you or set aside sale items you had your eye on. Let them work for you!

4) Invest in a good hairstyle. If you aren't crazy about your hair, be aware of women whose haircut and color are attractive. Ask them who they go to and make an appointment with their stylist.

5) There are three things that age a woman…her weight, her hair and her skin. Take care of all of them and you'll be an ageless, confident beauty!

Reading Resources:

What Not To Wear by Trinny Woodall and
    Susannah Constantine
Jackie: The Clothes of Camelot by Jay Mulvaney

Online Resources:

http://www.corporette.com
http://www.instyle.com
http://www.gilt.com

7
—— WHO IS THE BELLMAN? ——

I had just landed in D.C., grabbed a cab and checked into the Capitol Hilton.

As I unpacked the Armani suits, I could feel a wicked cold coming on. Ugh.

I thought about the next 24 hours.

Up at the crack of dawn, a 20-minute walk to wake the brain, room service that included a stiff jolt of caffeine, call home, take a cab to company headquarters, alive and perky at 7:30 a.m., endless meetings, an afternoon that included my major hour-long presentation and lively Q and A, call home, cocktail reception at 5:30, dinner with board, drinks after dinner with key board members, cab back to hotel, call home, up past midnight answering emails.

And a cold was taking over.

Never mind the next 24 hours—right now I had 15 minutes to get dressed and make it to the opening cocktail reception. But I needed to run to a drug store and get some zinc lozenges to stave off the cold. How could I get it all done?

My friend Denise arrived at my hotel room to pick me up. I was a bit frantic and said, "Go ahead without me. I'll be late. I'm unpacking and need to go to the drug store because

I have to stop this cold in its tracks."

Without missing a beat, she said, "Call the bellman. Give him $20 to go to Walgreens to get some zinc lozenges and have him deliver it to your room. He'll be delighted to have the cash and you'll get your medicine in 15 minutes."

I did just that. And it all unfolded as she predicted.

When the bellman arrived at my room 15 minutes later with the zinc lozenges, I was grateful for his great customer service and he was grateful for the chance to make $20 in 15 minutes. Denise looked at me with all her wisdom and said, "You're a lovely wife, wonderful mother and outstanding executive, but there are times when you don't have to do it all on your own. You need to ask, 'Who is the bellman? Who can help me and would be happy to accomplish the task before me?'" She was absolutely right.

Look at your to-do list today and ask, "Who is the bellman?"

THE LESSON:

To experience great success in your professional and personal life you must have a comprehensive support system surrounding you. As women, we multitask at an extraordinary level and we keep adding to our list of "things to do," when often, help is minutes away.

Do you remember the night I was consumed with fear and anxiety about my future? It was one of the toughest nights of my life.

I didn't know at that point that all options in one's personal and professional life are possible when one has a *comprehensive* support system in place. Each aspect of your support system, from family to child care to your home to a cherished group of friends, must be in place if you are to successfully integrate—and excel—in your personal and professional goals.

Ok, what does that comprehensive support system consist of?

Let's start with your family. Quite simply, family is complicated. If your parents and/or stepparents are still living you will get a lot of feedback from them filtered through their own life experiences that you'll have to deal with. If you are lucky, they will love you and be proud of you. But they will have lots of opinions, some of which you may not agree with.

Respect their opinions and be grateful for their love and good intentions. If their judgment or criticism is too much to bear, graciously set boundaries on the amount of time you spend discussing your life.

If you are married or in a long-term committed relationship, you will need the love and support of your partner. (Now that is an understatement!)

I once heard that in each intimate relationship there must

be two gardeners, with at least one gardener on duty each day to nurture and nourish the relationship. If heaven forbid neither shows up, the relationship will die.

When couples hit a rough patch, it's often because a huge transition occurs in one of the partner's lives and they both scramble to adjust to the new "norm."

As they both try to get their individual footing back to regain a balance in the relationship, a power shift can occur.

Power can shift in subtle and not so subtle ways. What can shift the power?

Money, for one. Our culture is driven to value money and the more you have, the more power you are perceived to hold. I'm not saying that is right or wrong, but our culture is built on capitalism and that means money. And our culture teaches our men that they must provide (that means making money) and protect their families. When there is a new influx of cash, a power shift inevitably occurs.

Time spent at work or traveling can shift power. A home, whether it's an apartment or a mansion, still needs to run smoothly for a family to prosper. If one in the couple is home and the other is away on a regular basis, household duties begin to fall to the one at home. Power shift.

Job changes for either partner require adjustments for a couple. A job promotion can cause as many adjustments as a layoff. Power shift.

Growing public visibility in a community, state or national spotlight can shift power. Suddenly the partner you see unshaven or in pajamas has a different public persona when dolled up and giving sound bites. Everywhere you go, one in the partnership is recognized and the other will begin to feel invisible. Power shift.

Changes in the mental or physical health of anyone in the family can shift power. When a family member is facing a health crisis, decisions must be made about family resources to address the crisis. Power shift.

Every time a transition occurs in a family unit you need the commitment of your spouse or partner that no matter what happens you'll have clear lines of communication and a desire to hold onto each other through the tough transitions. And I mean hold on tight because it can be a wild ride.

As a side note, one of the things that my husband Jeff did that really helped our marriage through transitions was his focus on us as a couple. Throughout 33 years of marriage Jeff has always planned special times for us just to be with each other. It could be as simple as a night out at a restaurant or more lavish like a weekend away. But in the crazy times juggling intense work schedules, family obligations and raising children it is so important to have reconnection time as a couple. It's one of the secrets of a long-lasting marriage. Both you and your spouse need to take time to be the "gardener."

You will also need a strong support system of friends. Friends come and go in our lives. The friends you had in high school or college are dear to you but they may not understand the nuances of your work life today. So as your career ramps up you need friends who are experiencing the same growing pains you are going through.

I was so very lucky to have two wonderful friends as my career took off. One was a peer in the company whose career path and mine were parallel for 25 years.

I met Denise Ivey when we were both invited to a career development session in D.C. She lived in Georgia and I in Iowa. When we entered the gleaming glass and chrome training room on the 26th floor of a high-rise overlooking the Potomac River, we spotted each other, struck up a conversation and have been fast friends ever since.

She is a brilliant critical thinker whose gift is to cut through the clutter, determine the most pressing issues and gather a team to execute the solution. I had a sixth sense about people and used that intuitive gene to strategically develop and then align people with the current and future needs of the organization. So we made a dynamic duo as we led our respective newspapers.

We talked on a regular basis, sharing business problems and brainstorming on solutions. We shared creative ideas and management tools and favorite books and a good laugh in every conversation.

It was a trusted friendship that still thrives today long after we have left the publishing industry.

The second friend was a peer in my community. Dr. Sylvia Gaffney was a trailblazer in a community that had few female leaders. A successful entrepreneur who is an expert in organizational transformation, she generously shared her expertise and wisdom with me. As a wife, mother and successful businesswoman Sylvia modeled how to "have it all" with a tenacious, vivacious and positive attitude. How lucky I am to call her my friend! It too is a trusted friendship that still thrives today long after we both moved from the community.

If you remember anything from this chapter remember this…*do not become isolated*. Don't shortchange your friendships. When you are juggling career, family, industry and community work it's easy to put friends on hold. But the result of a lack of supportive friends is isolation and insulation, which can ultimately lead to burnout.

The third source of support is your mentors, who in turn have a network. In my experience it appears that men tend to network shallow but wide and women tend to network deep but narrow. I think we could learn a lesson from our male colleagues. In the three communities in which I published newspapers, I had male community leaders who took me under their wings. I found these male mentors in a variety of ways. I found my first community male mentor when I joined a service club. My second male mentor sought me out. And I personally sought out my third male mentor. All three male community mentors shared great advice, introduced me and then gave me access to their deep networks. These networks were invaluable to the success of my career.

The fourth source of support surrounds your home. To maintain your energy level and manage your time, you'll need to find the "bellman" for the activities you can delegate to others. If you have a demanding job everyone in your family should be stepping up and participating in having the home run smoothly…from laundry to cooking to cleaning the bathroom. If you find that certain activities stress you out or deplete your energy, by all means give yourself permission to call in outside resources. The first support system I allowed myself was to hire a cleaning service. It took me a while to add this resource but when I did I wondered why it took me so long!

And you will need the support of your children.

By the way, your children's ability to adjust will amaze you. But if you are like every other mother I know you'll feel guilty at some point about how you are raising your children.

Here is a story to illustrate this point.

Our son Ryan was nine years old when our daughter Emma was born. Just as I had during my maternity leave with Ryan, I relished my time with Emma, basking in that unique rhythmic dance that mother and child create together. And once again when my maternity leave was drawing to a close the guilt pangs resurfaced.

Plus, my boss had begun calling me at home with a question here and a question there that implied, "You are needed back in the office. Now."

So I put the suit back on and left the quiet middle-of-the-night feedings to re-enter the hard and fast newspaper world. The guilt pangs continued each day as I put Emma into our babysitter's arms and gathered up Ryan to take him to school before heading to the office.

It was a particularly difficult morning when Emma was crying and not wanting to leave me that I got a jolt of wisdom from Ryan.

I had thrown my briefcase in the backseat and Ryan had climbed into the shotgun position in my car. As I was pulling out of the driveway, with Emma's cries still resonating in my mind, I turned to Ryan and confessed, "Ryan, I never stayed home with you and I've felt guilty about it all these years. I think I need to stay home with your baby sister."

Nine-year-old Ryan, with all his wisdom, reached across the front seat, gently placed his hand on my arm and simply replied, "Mom, you have a really good job. Go to work."

Wasn't that remarkable? Here I was absorbed in my feelings of motherly guilt while my young son knew instinctively that our family was thriving with plenty of positive, healthy child care support surrounding us.

Let's talk about the guilt. First, I don't care if you work outside the home or within the home, you will feel guilty. About *something*. It's as if buried in our DNA is a gene that carries guilt.

As 21st century women, we are lucky to live in a day and age in which every choice imaginable lies before us. But freedom without direction can breed anarchy. Within ourselves.

We veer down a path and when the first obstacle hits we begin to doubt the choices we have made. In an attempt to solidify our choices, we seek out information that validates our decisions. And there is plenty of information on any subject, whether it's work, home or personal relationships, much of it contradictory, and much of it causing more guilt and uncertainty.

If you are worried about the amount of time you spend at work, your neighbor will tell you that she just won "volunteer of the year" at her son's school. If you are contemplating cutting back your work hours, your college roommate will call to share news about her huge job promotion.

Comparisons will kill you, so stop that nonsense right now. Give up the guilt. It is not serving you. You may think it is motivating you but it's not. It's just making you feel lousy.

The old wisdom that there is a time and place for each season of our life is true. You are tooling along and life happens. Babies are born. Loved ones get sick. Your spouse loses his job.

I've long advised clients to imagine that one's career is on a dimmer switch. Sometimes the dimmer is on full power and lighting the way for ourselves and others. Sometimes it's scaled back to 75 percent to leave a reserve of energy for other aspects of your life. As the years go by you will toggle back and forth in response to life. Every season of our life has its place and pace.

Having children requires long-term thinking. Just about every woman I know had this thought when she found out she was pregnant or found out a child was entering the family: how in the world can I raise this child for the next two decades?

Men have the same response but the culture teaches them to laser focus on two aspects of child rearing: provide and protect. So if a man has a steady income and provides a home in a safe environment he is doing his job. For women it's much more complicated. Financial considerations are very important but she is also equally concerned about the emotional well-being of her children. Are they happy? Do they have friends? Are they accepted at school?

Of course men and women both care about the emotional well-being of their children, just as they both care about the financial security of the family. But we live in a capitalist society whose value rests on money. When life happens, men will go into overdrive on providing. Provide answers. Provide action. Provide income.

When life happens, women survey all the options.

You ponder, "Should I go or should I stay? How will this affect me and my family long-term?"

Here is the good news. If you love your job and believe your bosses and your company value your work, chances are you will stay. If you have a role model or have seen other women successfully juggle a life transition while working, chances are you will stay. If you have a good salary and benefits, chances are you will stay. If you have lots of support systems, both within your family and at work, chances are you will stay. If you have found good, affordable, accessible care for your children while you are working, chances are you will stay. If you see the long-term benefits of working for your organization, chances are you will stay.

But if any of those are a miss, seeds of doubt will grow and can cause a departure from the workplace. Which brings me to the very last support system…child care.

I've been working since my children were born so child care has been a part of life. Our family has experienced it all, from daycare to Montessori school to nannies to in-home care to au pairs.

I marvel at how much love these teachers and caretakers gave to our children and am grateful for the experiences we shared as a family.

To make it to the top of any profession you'll need the best child care you can provide for your children. I cannot under-score more that choosing your child care is one of the most important decisions you will ever make.

Don't make this decision in haste or when you are exhausted or on overload. You'll grasp at the first solution, which may not be the best answer.

Always listen to your gut. If you are interviewing a caretaker and sense something is a little off the mark, it is. In fact, it will amplify over time.

So if you have a gnawing sense that something isn't right, don't settle and think, "Oh if it doesn't work out I'll just change it down the road." Once you bring a child care provider into your family's life, new routines are established and it takes a lot of energy to disengage yourself and the family. And you'll need to start all over to find the right provider. Take that extra time up front to find the right solution. So here is your support system list: your family, spouse, friends, mentors, home care, children and child care providers.

Let go of your guilt, listen to your gut, and go for it. It's all right. Everything is all right, and with a support system in place, it will continue be all right throughout your life.

NEXT STEPS:

1) Answer these questions in your journal: Are your career dreams proactive or reactive? Quite simply, do you have the support you need to reach your greatest potential in the following areas of your life?

For each of these areas rate your support system on a scale of 1-5, with 5 indicating superb support and 1 indicating no resources:

    Family?
    Spouse?
    Friends?
    Mentors?
    Home maintenance?
    Children?
    Child care?

Review your ratings. Any areas with a 1-2 rating warrant serious support needed. For each of these areas ask, "Who is the bellman?"

2) If you are contemplating whether to stay home or go back to work ask yourself these questions:

Does the company or institution I work for value my work?

Is my work stimulating and fulfilling?

Is my salary helping my family prosper?

Do I have solid health care benefits?

Does my workplace offer a 401(k) that helps me save for my future?

Are my support systems strong enough to sustain me through the changes that occur with another child?

Evaluate your finances. What are the best child care options for your family short-term and long-term?

Reading Resources:

Passages by Gail Sheehy

Gift from the Sea by Anne Morrow Lindbergh

What I Know Now by Ellyn Spragins

Online Resources:

http://www.euraupair.com

http://www.drphil.com

8
— YOUR BODY NEVER LIES —

*O*ne of the many things I inherited from my mother is her boundless energy.

Unfortunately for the first few decades of my life I took my good health and remarkable energy level for granted.

So I found myself pushing the endurance levels and piling on more responsibility, which resulted in endless activities into an already jam-packed life.

Somewhere in my mid-forties the health piper had to be paid. I first noticed it with my sleep patterns. No amount of sleep would stave off the constant feeling of exhaustion.

This lack of deep sleep showed up with a perpetual deep wrinkle embedded between my eyes, while dark circles underneath couldn't be camouflaged by expensive makeup. Fortified by gallons of caffeine, I had lost my appetite.

Fortunately I had a friend who intervened.

We met every six months or so for lunch. She plopped down in the booth at our favorite restaurant one day, looked me straight in the eye and proclaimed, "Mary, I have found the fountain of youth!"

In her mid-50s she looked 35, so I was all ears. She proceeded to disclose details on her new doctor who specialized in female health care.

"No offense but you need her," she said. "You look like hell. That wrinkle between your eyes is the size of the Grand Canyon. And how much weight have you lost? You look like a scarecrow."

Thank God for good friends who aren't afraid to speak the truth! She whipped out her phone and called the doctor to make me an appointment. I was so exhausted at that point that I had no words to protest.

Four weeks later I entered the doctor's office.

What is it about a doctor's appointment that makes one try and buck up for one's best presentation? It's like washing your hair before seeing your hair stylist or dusting before a house cleaner arrives. I'd given it a valiant effort—makeup, some deep breathing, a perky smile—but there was no fooling this doctor. Throughout the exam she was profoundly smart, compassionate and intuitive. But she didn't hold back.

She looked me straight in the eye and said, "Your adrenals are shot."

Heck, I don't even know what an adrenal was, but I knew *something* in my body was shot!

As she laid out a comprehensive plan to get my body back in shape, a question floated across my mind…when was the last time I actually paid attention to what was going on in my body?

THE LESSON:

Your body never lies.

Let that sink in for a minute. Your body never lies.

Ok, so maybe right now you're sitting on an airplane or curled up in your favorite chair. Wherever you are I want you to put this book down (not right this second—you have an assignment!), close your eyes, take three long, deep breaths and pay attention to your body. Quiet the noise in your mind and concentrate on your body. For most of you this is going to be a very hard assignment because you spend so much time in your head that your body gets the short straw.

Starting at the top of your head, slowly do a scan of your entire body.

Do you get frequent headaches? Migraines?

The neck: Is it knot-free?

Shoulders: Do you stand straight or hunched over from far too many hours in front of a computer screen?

Chest: When was the last time you did a self-exam? Are you taking deep, nourishing breaths that bring energy and relaxation, or short, shallow breaths that leave you winded and anxious?

Stomach: Does your stomach gurgle from too many cups of caffeine when what your body wants is a healthy meal?

Do you suffer from chronic heartburn or sour stomach brought on by overeating, unhealthy food or stress?

Hips: Are you pain-free after a hearty walk?
Legs: Are they lean and strong and flexible?
Feet: Are the stilettos causing your toes to cramp?

Now here is the real question. Where do you store your stress?

Mine is in my gut and I learned to store my stress there long, long ago.

When I was growing up we marked our coming-of-age by the roles we were taking on. The scenario in middle America was something like this: graduate from high school, graduate from college, get married, start your fabulous career, have children and do all of the above with ease and grace. Oh and you're supposed to look hot, too.

Following the second wave of America's women's movement, women were taught they could not only have it all but should DO it all. So we bravely forged ahead. Because we could, we thought we should say "yes" to every opportunity that presented itself.

Armed with few role models, support systems or healthy

coping skills, we were not taught to self-edit frequent requests for our time, talent or treasure.

We didn't weigh the magnitude of the cumulative effect of those requests, so we had a difficult time determining the consequences of saying yes. "Yes" always seemed the appropriate answer.

Does this sound familiar? This is when "pile on" occurs.

Years ago when my stress level was in the stratosphere I had a visual image of my life as a jar filled with marbles. Each task I took on, each time I said "yes" when my heart said "no," each time I volunteered, each I time I took on the needs of others before I took care of my own needs first... each one of these tasks was a marble in the jar.

And I feared that the marbles would begin to spill out over the top of the jar and I would lose my marbles!

Thank God before that happened my gut began to act up. After doctors, procedures and prescriptions, the real remedy was quite clear. I needed to start making healthy food choices, say no more often to other people's requests and yes to being in tune with my body.

When I did just that, my gut stopped hurting and I could stomach life again.

Healthy food choices? You certainly don't need me to tell you what foods in the right proportions allow your body to best serve you.

Saying no more often? If work needs to get done a woman will often add it to her plate before "imposing" on others and asking for help. Suddenly one has a busy life instead of a full life.

But I recently heard a profound statement: "No" is a complete sentence. It's liberating when you say no more often to others' requests and yes to your own needs.

And even more freeing when you simply say no without any reason to explain how you could possibly say no. You don't owe anyone an explanation. "No" is good enough.

(OK…if you were raised in an ultra-polite family and you can't bear to just say "no," couch it like this: "That sounds interesting, however my schedule is already filled with commitments that I want to see through so I need to say no this time. I do wish you the best of luck.")

Here is another profound statement: I deserve to have my needs met.

If you find you are putting others' needs before your own, repeat that statement out loud and often until "no" becomes a more frequent part of your vocabulary.

And being in tune with your body? If I stress (!) it enough that you need to pay attention to what your body is telling you and then act on that information in a timely manner,

I guarantee that the stress in your body will be reduced and you'll live a longer, healthier life.

Stress lands some place in your body and consistently will attempt to start the conversation with you. It could be a cough that lands deep in your lungs long after the first cold symptoms subside. It could be a stomach ache every time you have to be in someone's presence. It could be an overall feeling of exhaustion each morning you wake up. Here is some critical advice:

1) Listen to your body early on and don't ignore its cues or try and will them away. Your body is trying to tell you something.

2) Look for two signs from your body: Does this linger? Does it recur?

3) Don't go for a quick fix. Look for the root cause.

4) Numbing the symptom with food, alcohol, tobacco or meds takes the edge off temporarily but the core problem will eventually need to be addressed.

Disease is dis-ease and starts when you tune out your body and stop observing. So back to our opening exercise. What is your body telling you?

If you have headaches, are you thinking too much and not acting enough?

If you have neck problems, are you being flexible?

If you have digestive problems, what is it you can't stomach?

If you have back pain, are you carrying too heavy a load?

If you have sciatic nerve problems, how are you dealing with someone who is a pain in the *!#&?

If you have leg problems, are you traveling in the right direction?

If you have feet problems, do you need to rest and be still?

Your body will never lie to you. Listen and don't ignore it.

NEXT STEPS:

How do you begin to listen to your body and say yes to its needs?

1) Do you love your primary care doctor? Is he or she really smart and able to connect the dots between all aspects of your health, including your dental care? Does he or she advocate for you with others within the health system? If not, find a new doctor.

2) Do you have quiet time each day to read, write, meditate or pray? If not, find it. Start with five minutes and add to it until you find the right amount of time that feeds your soul.

3) If you could change one thing about your diet, what would it be? Can you make that one change today and sustain the change for 21 days?

4) Do you have a form of exercise that works for you? If not, remember when you were a kid. What was your favorite form of play? Riding a bike? Hiking through the woods? Dancing to music? Playing soccer? Tap into your inner kid and find a physical activity that makes you smile.

5) Do you still smoke? If yes, get help from your doctor and quit.

6) Do you drink more than seven glasses of alcohol a week? If yes, cut back to a maximum of seven drinks per week.

7) Are you on any prescription drugs that no longer serve you? Discuss with your doctor how you can wean yourself off.

8) Can you fall asleep and sleep through the night? If not, put a routine in place to slow down before bedtime. Stop computer or TV stimulation 30 minutes before sleeping. Indulge yourself in a bath or quiet reading before sleeping.

9) Do you repeatedly drive too fast? Talk or text while driving? If yes, stop today.

10) Do you know where you store your stress? What is your body telling you?

Reading Resources:

Women's Bodies, Women's Wisdom by Christine Northrup, M.D.

Younger Next Year for Women by Chris Crowley and
	Henry S. Lodge, M.D.

8 Weeks to Optimum Health by Andrew Weil, M.D.

Online Resources:

http://www.realage.com

http://www.drnorthrup.com

http://www.womenshealthmag.com

9
—— ACT LIKE YOU BELONG ——

I'd been publishing the *Rockford Register Star* for four years and had been an officer of a Fortune 500 company for three when I got a call from the CEO of Gannett, who invited me to attend the Gridiron Club Dinner in Washington, D.C.

The Gridiron Club is an elite, invitation-only organization comprised of active members representing major newspapers, news services, magazines and broadcast networks. Its annual dinner, held each March, is attended by the President of the United States, his cabinet members, members of the Supreme Court, foreign ambassadors and congressional leaders from both parties.

The evening begins with a reception and dinner. After the U.S. Marine Band plays a medley, the Club proceeds with skits that lampoon one party and then the other.

The festivities end with a response by the President.

Yes, THE President.

So imagine this: 600 of the most powerful men in the country, dressed in tuxes, without their wives (spouses are not invited to the event), and a few dozen newswomen in the Capital Hilton ballroom. Including me.

One of my greatest mentors, Curtis Riddle, also attended that evening. Curtis is a handsome African American, and in those days he was often the only black person in the room, while I was often one of a handful of, if not the only, woman. When we appeared at industry functions together we were referred to as "the black and the broad."

So there Curtis and I were. As we walked into the ballroom, I paused to take in the moment.

I looked at Curtis.

He asked, "Are you nervous?"

I nodded yes.

He bent down and whispered in my ear, "Take a deep breath, kid, throw your shoulders back and *act like you belong.*"

As I walked confidently into the ballroom I was grateful that I could share one of the biggest nights of my life with one of my most influential mentors.

THE LESSON:

Find a mentor who not only guides you but has the power to promote you and open doors for you.

Now, what exactly does "mentor" mean to you?

For many a mentor is an experienced person entrusted with

the education of another. As our young protégé embarks on a new adventure, the mentor is a guide, a sounding board and a wealth of sage advice.

These are all great things. But the most valuable mentors are those who not only provide wise counsel but who can open doors, recommend you for more responsibility and fight for your advancement.

Remember the old saying, when the student is ready the teacher will appear?

Each of my mentors showed up at just the right moment when I was ready to fully understand and accept their unique leadership gift in my life. I've had many mentors but I'm compelled to tell you about these special people.

First is Sam Becker. He taught me to stretch outside of my comfort zone. When I arrived on the University of Iowa campus I loved studying theater, music, literature and art. I couldn't get enough. As fate would have it, Sam was assigned as my academic advisor. As we reviewed my upcoming semester's class load he recommended taking a business class. After lots of objections on my part, Sam convinced me that one day I just might need some marketing and advertising knowledge. These classes were my first exposure to a field I eventually pursued. Sam also helped me secure an internship at a fledgling radio station in town that eventually turned into my first full-time broadcasting job right out of college.

Not only did he believe in me, he gave me great advice and advocated on my behalf.

Second is Peg Fitzpatrick. When I was the advertising director of the WGN Companies, Peg recruited me into the newspaper business to oversee the sales staff of the *Iowa City Press-Citizen*. Peg not only taught me the newspaper business, she gave me free rein to run the sales department day to day. We met every night after 5:00 p.m. She asked great questions to help me come to my own management decisions. If I made a mistake, without criticism or judgment she'd ask me what happened and what I would do differently in the future. I marveled at her creative ideas, sales presentation skills and relationships with customers. She stretched me to learn all aspects of the business including the dreaded budgeting process. Within two years she was promoted to a larger newspaper and because she had invested in my development I was promoted into my first executive position. Once again, not only did she believe in me, she gave me great advice and she advocated on my behalf.

Third is Mike Coleman. Mike was my first regional newspaper boss. Charming and disarming, people couldn't help but like Mike. He was a class act. I would watch Mike in the diciest situations with community leaders, egomaniac executives or angry advertisers and I marveled at how he defused the situation and directed the outcome with a calm demeanor and a sense of humor. Mike taught me how to lead in a public arena with grace and class. I worked hard for Mike and was rewarded with his position when he moved on to more responsibility. Years later, long after he retired, he and his wife Mary Louise flew to Des Moines to surprise Jeff and me when we were being honored with a community service award. I was so touched by his continual support so many years later. He believed in me, gave me great advice and advocated on my behalf.

Fourth is Bill O'Donnell. The first week I arrived as publisher in Rockford, Bill was gracious to come to my office and welcome me and my family to our new community. A legendary leader in Rockford, he is a charming Irishman with a wicked sense of humor. What blew me away about Bill was his generosity in opening doors for a newcomer like me. Every few months Bill would organize and host a "no agenda" lunch with an interesting assortment of community leaders. From the local bishop to college presidents to the mayor to TV anchors to the local prosecutor, we broke bread with Bill O'Donnell and discussed every topic under the sun. It allowed me to personally get acquainted and build relationships with key community leaders in a relaxed and trusted setting. As a young woman, and an outsider at that, this was an enormous gift to me. Bill also has a deep faith and seemed to know just when I needed a word of encouragement. In some of my darkest hours a card or a book inscribed by Bill would arrive, giving me just the message I needed to hear to carry on. I once asked him about this and with that famous Irish twinkle in his eye, he responded, "My guardian angel talks with your guardian angel." I am so very lucky to have him as a mentor.

Fifth is Frank Vega. A street-smart guy from Tampa, Florida, Frank is the only person I've ever met who can use the "f" word as a noun, verb, adverb and adjective all in one sentence. He wasn't your typical corporate executive. But I'm not sure if I've ever met a leader who evoked the kind of loyalty that he created on his team. I once asked him about it and he said that everyone wants to believe that they are part of something big and grand. They want to understand how their contributions make a difference in the success of the company. He and his team worked hard and played hard. He taught me how to lighten up and laugh while leading. He believed in me, gave me great advice and advocated on my behalf.

Next is Gary Watson. No one had more of an impact on my career than Gary. For a long time Gary was my boss's boss. I never met anyone who knew the newspaper business as well as he did. He had a photographic memory. Astonishingly he could pull out facts and figures from documents or meetings from prior decades. There was no place to hide when you were in Gary's presence. You had to know your business and you had to get results. Gary promoted me, not on experience, but on potential, to a top publishing position when I was 30 years old. He promoted me again at 34. And he made me an officer in a Fortune 500 company when I was 36 years old. He taught me the importance of hiring the right people, getting them the resources to do their jobs and then getting out of the way. He taught me that when hiring people, if you have a choice between experience or smarts, always go with smarts. He taught me to pick my battles. Long before diversity was fashionable, he walked his talk in promoting people of all ages, races, sexual orientations and genders based on performance. I will never know the countless doors and opportunities he provided me. All I know is that I would not be living the life I have today without his support, knowledge, guidance and advocacy. I am very grateful to him.

Last is Curtis Riddle. You met Curtis at the beginning of this chapter and I end with him because Curtis taught me how to lead from the heart. As one of the (if not *the*) most powerful and accomplished African American newspaper executives in the country, Curtis taught me to be confident and centered in my leadership even when faced with hostility or prejudice. But his most important lesson for me came within days of working for him.

I had accepted the position as publisher in Rockford. My family was in transition. Jeff was still working in Iowa City and I needed to get four-year-old Ryan settled into his new town. My job had always required travel but I was very concerned about being out of town while Ryan was adjusting to all these changes. Curtis had just been promoted to a huge new job and he was my new boss. In our first one-on-one meeting I leveled with him. I told him I had never asked the company for any adjustment in my work schedule but with my family responsibilities I needed to be relieved of travel duties for six months. He didn't hesitate. "I understand, Mary," he said. "We'll work around it." For six months he lived up to his side of the bargain, conducting regional meetings in Rockford so I didn't have to choose between the needs of my family and the needs of the job. I know he had to make significant adjustments in running the region to accommodate my needs during that time. But he never complained and never made me feel guilty. In fact, he never brought it up.

When those six months were up I went back out on the road. But my loyalty to Curtis was ferocious. To this day I would do anything for that dear man.

Curtis taught me that leading is about building trust and loyalty with those you are entrusted to lead.

He taught me that leadership isn't about others adjusting to you but rather you adjusting to your team to bring out their best. He taught me that like marriage, leading is equal measures of give and take.

Most importantly he taught me to lead from the heart.

As you can see, I had some pretty amazing mentors. They came in all sizes and shapes but when I was ready they appeared.

You might be ready for a mentor to appear, so how can you attract that right person into your life?

That's where *you* come in.

To attract a mentor you need to take the initiative. Go the extra mile. Shine brighter. Show your mentor that you are striving to live beyond your potential.

When a person sees another with great potential they are naturally drawn to help them. They think, "Wow, if I could buy stock in that person I would."

Would others want to buy stock in you? If the answer is yes, they are banking on your potential and you are the perfect candidate to attract the right mentor into your life.

If not, others are not seeing the potential inside you. Why is that? Your effort? Your attitude? Your results?

Most mentors are enormously generous by nature, however, everyone wants to see an upside to their investment.

Remember that mentoring is a give-and-take process. Your mentor advises, teaches and advocates for you. How can you reciprocate? First of all help your mentor achieve his or her goals. Be respectful. Be grateful. Thank your mentor on a regular basis, now and in the future, for the generous gift of self that he or she has given you. Share your experiences and expertise with your mentor. Be a great ambassador and make your mentor proud.

I learned long ago that mentoring multiplies. Once you receive mentoring and grow from it, you can reciprocate and be a mentor yourself. In the end, the greatest gift you can give your mentor is to honor his or her legacy by paying it forward.

It's exhilarating to have a mentor but far more rewarding to be a mentor and know that you have changed lives by believing in others, sharing your wisdom and opening doors. You may never know how an encouraging word or a simple introduction can change a life, but taking that extra step can reap untold dividends for another for generations to come.

NEXT STEPS:

1) What specifically are you looking for in a mentor? Is it knowledge? Advice? Contacts? Opportunities?

2) Are you attracting mentors into your life? If not, why not?

3) Ask a trusted confidant, is it your effort? Attitude? Results?

4) What can you give back to your mentor that helps them achieve their goals?

5) Are you living up to your potential? Beyond it?

6) Are you willing to pay it forward?

Reading Resources:

Work with Passion by Nancy Anderson

Influencer by Kerry Patterson, Joseph Grenny, David Mayfield, Ron McMillan and Al Switzler

The M-Factor by Lynne Lancaster and David Stillman

Online Resources:

http://www.jimcollins.com

http://www.businessweek.com

http://www.vocationvacations.com

10
——LEADING BY THE 3 C's——

*A*fter years of planning, Jeff and I bought land out in the Illinois countryside and built our dream home.

We had watched over each detail and carefully selected each feature. One of our favorite things was the screened-in porch on the back of the house.

Late one summer night, soon after we moved in, we were sitting on the porch listening to the crickets when two-year-old Emma squealed, "What is that?"

I looked out over the lawn to see a small army of fireflies lighting up our back acre of land.

Grabbing her hand, she and I ran out into the grassy area and stood in the middle of the light show. We slowly twirled together, taking in the symphonic melody of the crickets and the flickering lights of the fireflies.

Emma pulled away. And after reaching out with precision timing, she caught a firefly in her hand.

"Look, Mom, look what I caught!" she cried out.

I believed the firefly would be crushed by the strength of her tiny fist and ran to her. Slowly, however, Emma unfolded her fingers, and we saw the firefly's light still glowing to the beat of the crickets.

But when she saw the tiny insect in her hand, she clenched her fist again. "Emma, not so rough," I said. "Here, let me help you. The firefly needs space to breathe. Open your fist. Talk to it. See, it wants to share its bright light with you."

Had I shouted out an angry "No!" to Emma she would've taken off running, or, being a two-year-old, maybe even done the exact opposite of what I asked. But when I spoke with her and clearly explained why she needed to open her fist, she willingly relaxed her grip. Together we watched the tiny creature's bright light come back to life.

THE LESSON:

Women's natural strengths—communication, collaboration and compassion—are perfectly aligned with the leadership skills needed today. *Now* is the time for women to join the highest ranks of leadership in the world.

I studied communication in college and have had a ringside media seat for years. I've always believed that the speed at which communication occurs is the speed at which not only an organization changes but an entire culture changes.

And speed? In our crazy world we have evolved from the farm to the factory to Facebook in record time.

What does that all mean for women in business?

For centuries our organizational structures have been set up like a triangle or pyramid.

The highest-ranking officer sits at the top of the organization. For example in a corporation the top spot is the chief executive officer. Underneath the CEO are the next highest-ranking officers, which in a corporation would be the vice presidents. Underneath the VPs are the managers. Underneath the mangers are the supervisors. And underneath the supervisors, God love them, are the workers. Each step down the pyramid represents less power.

You'll see this structure in just about every kind of organization because it has been enormously efficient and quite effective for centuries. However, communication in a pyramid organization is very linear. The top dog makes a statement and this filtered communication travels down through the layers of the organization with a limited ability for the rank and file to respond or affect its outcome.

But a crazy thing happened at the end of our last century. The Internet blew apart how humans communicate. The exploding digital space brought power to the individual voice. When massive change occurred in communication, entire industries were disrupted. Unfortunately this digital disruption happened in the midst of one of our planet's toughest economic cycles. And with it went jobs.

Many CEOs, scrambling to save their businesses, consolidated or eliminated positions and began to gut the layers within their organizations. Gone were layers of middle management. The space between top management and the worker dwindled. Communication, fueled by an emerging digital space, leveled one-way linear communication in an organization and was replaced with employees and customers weighing in with their opinions, ideas and knowledge during the decision-making process.

No longer sacrificing silence for security, individuals within organizations and nations are now using their voices to impact and influence their future.

Leaders have always needed to be strong communicators. But leaders now must communicate in a transparent world and must value the open conversations that are occurring internally and externally around the organizations they lead.

It's one thing to listen and engage in robust conversation. It's quite another to actively use this information in decision-making. And so a second needed leadership skill is emerging: collaboration. Today's work force expects to be heard, engaged and valued in the decision-making process. Leaders and followers are sharing information and are active partners together.

With open communication and collaborative work environments, the third leadership skill to emerge is compassion. It's pretty tough to ignore a voice in need or a voice of reason and not open one's heart and mind to a new possibility. With compassion comes better decisions for the greater good.

So the new emerging leadership skills of communication, collaboration and compassion—the 3 C's—are vital to leading the next generations of citizens and workers.

But what strikes me is how once again communication is shaping the ways in which we not only lead our organizations but how our organizations are structured. The pyramid structure, with its hierarchy of power and control, is no longer being tolerated or trusted as the best means of governance.

A new structure is emerging, shaped by how we communicate. It's the circle.

Let's take a look at a simple form of communication today.

Let's say you've been reading this book on an airplane. You pack everything up, de-plane and head out into the terminal. You turn on your phone, go to your Facebook account and post a comment: "I'm reading Mary Stier's new book." Within seconds you receive posts on your Facebook wall. In my fantasy example the posts say such things as, "I loved that book. Especially the chapter on power!" or "I knew her when she published the *Register*," or "I heard her speak recently. If you ever get the chance ask her to tell the story about the

Deep End."

Within minutes you have an assortment of thoughts, ideas and opinions that have traveled around the globe attracting bits and pieces of information that all arrive back to its source...your original post.

But your singular piece of information has now been transformed by the ideas, thoughts and opinions of others.

And so it is with the new organizational circular structure. The new leader, aligned with communication, collaboration and compassion, welcomes different ideas, listens intently to those he or she serves, and includes differing thoughts, ideas and opinions into the decision-making process.

This doesn't mean, of course, that there is no one at the helm. Our new leader is still responsible for creating and articulating a vision, synthesizing and adjudicating input, making final decisions, holding others accountable and getting results. But she or he utilizes the 3 C's to create and implement ideas that contribute to the organization as well as its individual members.

In a new world with robust communication, I am struck by how women are particularly wired for the leadership skills that are demanded in this changing leadership landscape. So many women are natural communicators, value the collaborative decision-making process, and have deep compassion in their hearts.

Now is the time, my friends, to step up and assume the helm of leadership in a world that desperately needs the wisdom and grace of women's leadership.

You have in your hands 10 ways to strengthen your personal leadership. You have the keys to open many doors for yourself and others.

Key in hand, why not start with your own door?

Unlock the door to *you*.

When the door is open, take a look at each of your unique gifts that you and only you can offer this world. Cast the doubts away and silence the old tapes that say it can't be done.

Embrace that potential deep inside of you. Go for it. Raise your hand. Take the risk. Use your voice. Get focused. Nurture your sense of humor. Take control of your life. Develop your style. Respect your body. Build support systems. Find your mentors. Mentor others. Assume the leadership reins.

You deserve it and the world needs it. Women are particularly adept at the skills needed to lead in today's environment. Could there be a better combination?

And remember my friends, never, ever give your power away to someone or something and wait for it to be given back to you. It's your power.

I will watch with anticipation and delight as your light transforms the leadership of the world as we know it.

NEXT STEPS:

1) Do you recognize your strengths in communication, collaboration and compassion? In what ways can you use this strength to realize your dreams?
   Communication?
   Collaboration?
   Compassion?

2) In your sphere of influence, how can you begin to structure your team into a circle?

3) What strengths do each of your team members exhibit and how can you align their responsibility with their strengths?

4) Turn to a fresh new page in your journal to write YOUR STORY. Ask yourself these questions:

What makes my life unique?

What do I know now that others don't know yet or haven't experienced?

What lessons can be learned from my life experiences?

What do I do easily and naturally without effort?

What do people tell me that I'm very good at?

What energizes me?

What consumes me?

What lights me up and lights my fire?

Reading Resources:

Leadership is an Art by Max DePree

Go Put Your Strengths to Work by Marcus Buckingham

The Art of Possibility by Rosamund Stone Zander and
        Benjamin Zander

Online Resources:

http://www.strengthsfinder.com

http://www.hbr.org

—— *Acknowledgments* ——

I am grateful for the love and support of so many who helped make this book possible:

To Denise Ivey who read the first chapter and insisted I write nine more. Your wise and wonderful counsel is a gift to me.

To Catherine Knepper whose guidance and editing over the past year was my compass.

To the team at Sigler Companies who worked tirelessly to produce the book in record time.

To Mark Marturello whose artwork always captures the essence of an idea and makes it come alive.

To my colleagues at the Gannett Company, Inc. who made the journey memorable.

To my clients and students who teach me every day.

To my girlfriends who anchor me.

To my sisters who make my heart smile.

To Jan and Jim who taught me the depth of family loyalty.

To Mom and Dad who are the greatest mentors in my life.

And most of all to my family…

To my daughter Emma for inspiring me to write the book.

To my son Ryan who gave a name to *Lady Leader*.

And to my husband Jeff. Life is so much more fun with you by my side.